FOCUS

FOCUS

How Your Energy Can
Change the World

NANCY BURSON

ibooks

NEW YORK
www.ibooks.net

DISTRIBUTED BY SIMON & SCHUSTER, INC.

An Original Publication of ibooks, inc.

Distributed by Simon & Schuster, Inc.
1230 Avenue of the Americas, New York NY 10020

ibooks, inc.
24 West 25th Street
New York, NY 10010

The ibooks World Wide Web Site Address is:
http://www.ibooks.net
ISBN: 0-7434-9326-5
First ibooks edition October 2004
Edited by Judy Gitenstein
Cover art by Nancy Burson
Cover design by Nancy Burson and Jay Vita
Printed in the U.S.A.

Contents

Introduction

Focus *verb*

to concentrate attention or energy

IT IS SAID THAT THE MORE DIFFICULT OUR LIVES
are, the more chances there are for spiritual develop-
ment. There is no doubt that our world today is a
potentially dangerous place. The threat of nuclear-
weapons use is real and constant. Threats of the
release of biological weapons are just as real. How do
we get beyond the fears of our new lives in this new
world of ours? There are 40-50 million people currently involved in what some call the "Spiritual
Awakening Movement." Let us all focus and together
we can help. Peace lies within each of us. This book
can guide you.

To change the world we must change ourselves,
and that's where we must begin.

Derek O'Neill's meditation produced a powerful phenomenon, shown here as shafts of light that appeared in the photograph taken by his wife, Linda, outside the Brooklyn Public Library. Derek is seated second from left.

ONE

Find Your Defining Images

WHEN I LECTURE AND TEACH, ONE OF THE FIRST stories I like to relate to my students concerns the power of our defining moments—the images that impact our lives.

About 15 years ago, a couple was having lunch at McDonalds. The woman, facing the front of the restaurant, noticed a suspicious-looking man pacing back and forth by a car parked outside. She urged her husband to turn and look, and he did for 2-3 seconds. Later, he will spend 40 minutes under hypnosis describing in detail the man he has seen. He will identify the pacer as the car-bomber on the FBI's Most Wanted List. Based on his description, a sketch artist was able to create an image and the FBI was able to identify the perpetrator.

According to the sketch artist, who I knew from working with the FBI's computer graphics lab, the doctor who had conducted the hypnosis said to the subject, "You're sitting in McDonalds eating, and your wife asks you to turn around, and so you do." The man, under hypnosis, turned around and the doctor said, "Now, freeze-frame that image." The man sat with his head turned for 40 minutes, describing in detail the bomber. At most, this man had only seen this criminal for only a few seconds.

"Freeze-frame that image," the doctor had said.

We are, all of us, compilations—composites, if you will—of all the images in our lives.

The first step in achieving focus in our lives is to find our defining images. Once we have identified the defining images we will be able to examine them so that we can focus on the positive images and cancel negative thoughts. We can also see which of our defining images from childhood we recreate through-out our lives. This awareness of our defining images is the first step toward consciousness. Then we can understand how we are all part of the bigger picture.

How do you find your defining images? Often if we close our eyes, the images that define us will appear. Use your closed eyes like a screen. See what comes up on your screen in front of you. What are the recurring images? Which are positive and which negative? The ones we attempt to push away are sometimes the most important to us.

What are the messages we repeat to ourselves over and over again on a daily basis? If we sit quietly, we can hear them. Are they positive or negative?

Once we have brought these images and/or messages into our consciousness we can examine them, discuss them openly with those we trust, and begin to learn from them. Relax and sit quietly. You can use any sort of meditation or visualization you like. Or simply, close your eyes and ask what you're here to learn. This is our homework, and we must all do it in order to shift forward in our lives.

Composites

All of us are the accumulation of our freeze-framed images. Our power, or lack of it, is a result of those pictures stored in our brain databases. Often we are unaware of which images will impact us later. Some of these images stored in our data bases nurture and heal us, while others have the power to weaken and destroy us. Each of us thinks at least 65,000 thoughts a day. If those thoughts are based on negative images, then the messages we are repeating to ourselves are negative as well. Our goal as conscious human beings is to create a tape that is constantly updating to include the positive, healing images and process-out the negative, toxic images.

My "compositology theory" evolved from a discussion I once had with my first publisher. When I asked my editor why he thought people would be interested in my book called Composites, he said, "Because we are all composites." (*Composites: Computer-Generated Portraits* was published in 1986 by Beech Tree/ William Morrow.)

A few years later I had a clear demonstration of compositology when I was pushing my son in a stroller up Broadway. In the space of ten minutes, I ran into two people I knew. The first told me how much my child looked like me. The other offered that my son looked exactly like my husband.

No one ever agrees on faces and this is part of their ability to fascinate. The most obvious thing about

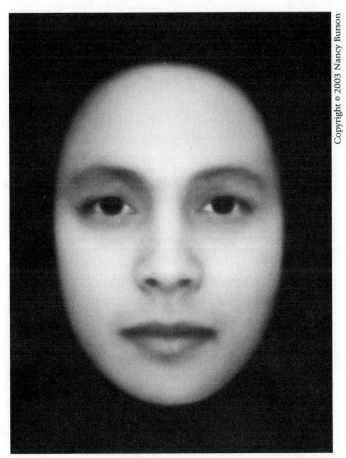

Mankind 2003, a computer-generated composite, taken from database images from The Human Race Machine, weighted to current world population and gender statistics.

seeing ourselves as composites is that most certainly, we are composites of our parents. We combine their physical selves as well as their essential selves—what they look like and who they are.

Second, we are all molecular composites in that all the atoms in our bodies were once a part of stars.

Third, all of us are composites of our emotions. It's an aspect of being human that enables us to be fearful and courageous simultaneously. And fourth, as we grow older, we become composites of our previous decades plus our present. Ultimately, if you're in acceptance of the concept of reincarnation, as a third of us on our planet do, then we are also composites of our previous lives as well.

What is our biggest job in life? Isn't our biggest job loving ourselves? What a hard time we humans have looking in the mirror each morning. How we all suffer, even if good hair days help periodically.

Many of us grew up with images that were so painful to us that as adults, they continue to undermine our lives, affecting all of our intimate relationships. We bring the fear we felt as children into our adulthood and it is expressed in the form of low self-esteem and self-sabotage.

Some of My Defining Images

I moved to New York City in 1968. I decided to pursue an idea I had to instantly reflect viewers' faces 25 years into the future. In the late '70s I collaborated with MIT, exploring ways a computer could transform live images of people from a camera. This early research, which I patented in 1981, resulted in what has since come to be called "morphing." The age-updated techniques for both children and adults that my former husband David Kramlich, and I developed have brought many missing children home, and many criminals to justice. Finding that first child was truly a transcendent moment. It was then that I understood that, for me, "art" needed to have some purpose . . . it needed somehow to give something significant back to the viewer.

I spent seven years photographing children with facial deformities and adults with faces distorted by disease. These were people who in spite of their disease or deformity were healed, whole . . . beautiful. It is my privilege to know them and love them. They have mastered the art of self-acceptance. Ours was a collaboration based on mutual trust and it felt even bigger; it felt like a step toward the education of a society that celebrates sameness and is distrustful of difference.

It was a step toward my own education, too. Perplexed and frustrated that the medical community had been unsuccessful in treating my immune problems and low-grade fevers, I went to visit a hands-on healer in 1995. Little did I know that this was the beginning of my own incredible journey. From my first visit to an "energy healer," I was convinced that what I had experienced was real and that what I had seen and felt must somehow be explainable. More importantly, my health began to improve immediately.

In 1995 I began photographing healers with the idea that if I could capture their energy on film, it would be significant not only to me, but to others. I began by using a Holga camera, a plastic camera with a plastic lens, because I felt somehow that the uncoated plastic lens might reveal more "energy" than a regular glass lens of a standard camera. Between 1995 and 2002, there were at least a dozen instances in which the effects seen in my pictures could not be explained (as far as I was concerned, and my photo lab agreed) as anything other than energy.

One of the most impressive early instances of

phenomena I caught on film occurred in 2000 when I photographed Gary Douglas. The photo session was audio taped by his assistants and it was in the same moment that he told me to "not be surprised if I find something irregular on my film" that an orange streak of light appeared over his heart in one of my photos.

I am awed by these miracles my camera is producing for myself and others to see. To me, these images carry direct messages from Source or Spirit. What they say is here is the evidence that energy exists. Show them to people knowing that no one will be able to prove that they are fake. Discount that coming from me, one of the pioneers of digitally manipulated photography, people may have problems accepting them. Trust that they will become part of the evidence that the paradigm shift is real.

Image: September 11, 2001

Living 16 blocks from the World Trade Center was, on September 11, 2001, literally a shake-up call as well as a wake-up call. I had thought my shaking building was yet another earthquake that New York City experiences periodically. And then there was the first phone call. I remember that my first reaction was that as a healer and minister, I should go down and offer my services. And my second thoughts were, I should go take pictures, and then I remembered my images are about healing, not horror. And then, as the scenario worsened that morning, I had listened to David (who, at the time, lived several blocks farther downtown than I do) break down on the phone in an emotional moment like I'd never witnessed in all 20 years I'd known him. Ultimately, what became most important on September 11 was my responsibility as a parent, and I waited for David to go and retrieve our child from school.

The images that stand out in my mind in the aftermath are based on my (then) 12-year-old son's reactions in the days that followed. I had watched him stab endlessly with a pocket knife at the two cardboard boxes left from the previous day's water delivery. He was going to get those guys and he was going to kill bin Laden if no one else did it before he was old enough. And that was a promise.

It was on the afternoon of September 12 that the wind shifted and suddenly the smell of the burning World Trade Center ruins was omnipresent. I had thought there was a horrible fire somewhere and I had opened the door of my loft and stepped into the hallway and said, "what's that burning? There is a fire somewhere." And my neighbor came out into the hallway and said, "that's it." And I said, "Oh, God really?" This was the smell that lingered and was to drift through our lives for the next three months.

The smell, the toxicity, I often described as one-part metal, one-part burnt electrical wiring, and one-part human. We did not open our windows for three months. I remember the walk to pick up my son from school two days later—necessary at the time due to the fact that our home in SoHo (named for the area south of Houston Street) was still part of "the zone"—above Canal Street, but below 14th Street, where there was still no transportation. I had torn a sock apart and used it for a mask over my face to keep out the fumes. After a search of downtown drug stores, we purchased the last box of sterile masks left in lower Manhattan, giving what we could to others attempting to find them. Almost everyone I saw on the street was wearing one kind of mask or another and in the weeks that followed and anthrax threatened, the usual street vendors outside our home on Broadway switched from purses to gas masks. It was surreal. The smell of the continuously burning Pit was especially present in the evening and early morning hours, and my son went to school periodically with a mask on for the next three months.

And what about the months that followed? What makes it hard to live in lower Manhattan is the constant reminder of what used to be and isn't now. Every time I head south outside my building, it's difficult to not recall what was there for so long before. Yet, if I head north, it's a normal day and the Empire State Building still rises majestic over midtown. It is the cockeyed landscape that constitutes the new downtown Manhattan that is yet to regain its balance. It is a constant reminder of our new lives. A friend of mine who lived in a high-rise on 8th Street has moved, worn down by the forever-changed cityscape outside his window. He wanted a view that didn't remind him of loss.

Two years later, 9/11 remains our downtown communities' collective defining image. Here there are thousands of witnesses whose lives are still encumbered by the trauma of seeing in real-time the images the rest of America saw on TV. Many of us traded in tears for resentment and rage held within.

I sat alone on the evening of Sept. 12 with my son safely at his father's for the night, and as I settled in on my usual place on the sofa, my comfort and prayerful place I call my power spot, I shivered and cried tears of what was to come of my adopted though seemingly permanent home of the past 33 years. I knew people who had lost their homes and offices, and I knew photographers and businesspeople who had escaped, I didn't know anyone that had actually fallen to their death. For that I felt blessed.

In the weeks that followed the attacks, two different New York Cities came into being. In the uptown New York, everything seemed normal more-or-less. People were numb and frightened, but their noses weren't challenged by toxicity and they hadn't been displaced from their homes.

The biggest loss was that New York City would never feel secure, and fear would forever coexist with joy living in the capital of the world. An insecurity about the future—the possibility of further attacks and further destruction—is reinforced on a continuing basis on the evening news. As I sat in my prayer room in the mornings after September 11, I would hear simultaneously the sound of my neighbor's doves and military jets flying overhead.

We are privileged, we downtowners, we independent artists. We've been handed a lot of homework to do, more than most Americans. And most of us have chosen to stay here because it is our homes and business and studios. We have taught in the colleges and universities, fallen in love, and built our careers here. It is here that we've formed a community and raised our children. When one is truly at home, there is no other place to go. So when someone asks me if I think about moving outside the city, my answer is "where would I go?" I still love it right where I am.

A few days after 9/11, I found myself visiting a friend who lives a few blocks from the World Trade Center site. It was my first real opportunity to witness the site firsthand. There were no cars allowed on the streets and people observed from barricades and railings that had been set up all around the site. Most impressive were the personal markings and messages of grief and hope on brown-and-white paper covering the barricades which stretched for blocks. Smoke still rose high up from various places within the rubble and a huge flag hung on one of the buildings adjacent to the site. I remember thinking that flag was a good thing, an appropriate and even grand thing to be there. But I also thought, I wonder what else there could be other than that? The answer, for me, came about seven months later when I focused on what I felt New Yorkers, especially downtown New Yorkers, needed to shift their lives and their grief forward. The answer was to "Focus on Peace."

Today, the largest multiplex cinema closest to my home is still the one at Battery Park, which overlooks the northeast corner of the World Trade Center site. It is ironic that this is sometimes where my family goes to be entertained. By the wall-length window of the theater complex there are a few video games that my son has been drawn to from time to time. One day early last year I couldn't help pointing out that the war game he was playing was the Simulacra, the simulation. The real thing was located over his shoulder, and all he had to do was turn his head to the right to see the real battleground in a most bizarre war.

Past and Present

In this post-9/11 world, the images from our past collide with our present. Again, we are frightened. Those of us who experienced the Cuban Missile Crisis remember the few days that there was the threat of nuclear war. We remember how teachers taught us to get down under our seats if the Emergency Broadcast System went off. We remember the jokes about what you really do in case of nuclear attacks. (You bend down, put your head between you legs and kiss your ass good-bye!)

Once we recognize how easy it is to differentiate and trade in the negative images for the positive ones, we can begin to ask ourselves the bigger questions:

- Am I ready to shift the negative images?
- Can I let go of these negative images and replace them with love in my heart?
- When do I want to be happy?
- What am I not seeing? How do I deal with these issues? What do I have to do to move on from here?
- What did I learn from this experience? What lessons am I here to learn today, and what am I here to learn for my whole life?
- What is my bigger picture?

How do we know if we're ready? If you picked up this book, you're already in alignment and agreement with its principles that your life can potentially be different than it is now. If happiness were simply about making money, all the wealthy people we know would be happy, and they're not. It's how we love that determines the quality of our lives, and that only begins with the core love for who and what we are ourselves.

TWO

Decide What You Want

SINCE THE 1960S, PHYSICISTS WORLDWIDE HAVE studied whether human beings could exert an effect on computers. What these experiments found was that human beings sitting in front of a computer were able to affect the outcome of an experiment with their thoughts. By using random number generators, which measured randomness with a volume of randomly generated numbers, it was found that human consciousness, through ordinary people, had the power to shift an outcome.

One hundred and fifty studies of human trials on healing conducted between the 1960s and '80s had all been shown to have a significant effect. Those successful studies were as diverse as speeding up gerbils, to protecting human red blood cells, and from healing the wounds of mice, to changing the molecular structure of water. What was also discovered was that the larger the organism, the greater the effect. The humans who needed healing the most would get the most effect, and the effect on yourself was only slightly less than the amount you could influence others. Be careful what you wish for, these studies seem to say. We create our own reality.

Each of us can make a difference if we focus on what we truly want.

Global Consciousness

Many books and studies and at least one PBS-television documentary serve as documentation for the SRI (Stanford Research Institute) experiments financed by the CIA on "remote viewing." The program was co-founded in 1972 by two physicists, Hal Puthoff and Russell Targ. Ending in 1995, it became the largest spy program to use clairvoyance as its base. What the remote viewing experiments showed was that normal people could learn how to "see" remotely, finding objects and places simply by focusing or "tuning in." More interesting still was the fact that the people who learned remote viewing had the ability to locate things in the past or the future as well.

You can test your own "psi," or psychic ability. It is, after all, a form of connectedness. You can practice remote viewing with friends by placing something unusual in a box and having them guess what's inside. You become more proficient at tuning in to an object simply by practicing. Always stick with your immediate first thought or impression. Don't think, just know.

You can also practice remote viewing by focusing on a location. Take a photo from a magazine or the travel section of a newspaper. Place it in an envelope, unfolded, and ask friends for their impression of the enclosed image.

Dr. Roger Nelson is the researcher who is the head of the Global Consciousness Project (GCP). It is an outgrowth of his work at the Princeton Engineering Anomalies Research (PEAR) Lab at Princeton University. The GCP is an international collaboration created in 1998 to study the reach, or scope, of human consciousness. They maintain a network of random event generators (REGs) with devices in more than 60 locations worldwide. They're called Electrogaiagrams, or EGGs, because they are designed to register coherent mental activity on the earth, much like an electroencephalograph, which measures the brain. The EGGs produce random numbers, or numbers without a pattern, the equivalent of flipping coins electronically. In the five years they have been functioning, they have formed non-random patterns many times. An early example was the funeral of Princess Diana, and the most powerful time measured, began in the morning of September 11, several hours before the World Trade Centers were struck. Roger Nelson, first and foremost a scientist, still searches for mechanisms that would explain his data other than a form of global consciousness at work, but he hasn't found any.

Recently, using data from 122 random events, Nelson's overall conclusion has odds-against-chance at one in a million. Here, science and statistics are providing us clear evidence that in fact, we are all profoundly connected.

Dr. Dean Radin, a research psychologist, has been using random pictures selected by a computer to discover that his subjects' bodies respond to emotional versus calm pictures before they were even shown to them. These experiments, which show the results of shifts in physiological responses, have been repeated with similar results in European experiments as well.

In *The Field*, Lynn McTaggart's book that synthesizes the evolution of quantum physics research into a cohesive whole, she states "the physicists had provided evidence that all of us connect with each other and the world at the very undercoat of our being." Through scientific experiment they'd demonstrated that there may be such a thing as a life force flowing through the universe-what has variously been called collective consciousness, or as theologians have termed it, the Holy Spirit.

Prayer

Much has been written about the effectiveness of prayer and long-distance healing, and the past few years have not been an exception. There have been significant studies regarding prayer efficiency, even for those unaware that they were being prayed for.

This explains why 79 of the nation's 125 medical schools now offer courses on prayer and spirituality. One significant new study comes out of Columbia University, in which a group of infertile women in Korea were unknowingly prayed for by people from the United States, Canada, and Australia. The pregnancy rate was 50% higher in the prayed-for group.

Prayer has been found just as effective on nonhumans in studies involving the healing of surgical wounds on mice and the growth rate of microbes in test tubes.

In a paper published in 1995 in *Scientific American*, David Chalmers, a Ph.D. from the University of Arizona, asserted that there is a large body of evidence suggesting that consciousness is a fundamental element of the universe, like energy. It is the way to explain the science of "intercessionary prayer," the term used to refer to individuals being prayed for by others.

If you don't believe in the efficacy of prayer, then it's unlikely you'll have the appropriate feelings that make prayer work. And the same applies to "petitionary prayer," or prayers for yourself.

My mother was Jewish but grew up in a Catholic neighborhood in St. Louis. My father's father was Jewish, and his mother was born gentile, but was later adopted by Jewish parents. After my parents divorced, my father married a Christian woman and became outspokenly anti-Semitic. It was not until my last visit with him before he died that he revealed the source of that anti-Semitism. His classmates at Princeton, it seemed, had ridiculed him for being a

Jew. Ironically, since he chose to be buried beside his parents in a Jewish cemetery, his Christian funeral had to be followed by a Jewish graveside service to comply with cemetery laws.

Christmastime at our house was celebrated with a large tree, and often there was the lighting of Chanukah candles, along with baked ham for dinner. It was all an eclectic blend. We were not very Jewish, we Midwestern Reform Jews. My brother and I were confirmed, not bar-mitzvahed. Our rabbi wore what looked more like a cowboy hat than a yarmulke. Still, after confirmation, I was an assistant in the Sunday school kindergarten, and I had a very active, very secret spiritual life. I would lie in my bed reciting prayers to myself every night . . . Christian prayers and Jewish ones . . . all that I knew by heart. I would pray myself to sleep.

My son is 15 now and his faith is eclectic. I remember when he was 7 years old and on a plane trip, he looked out the window and noticed the rays of light shining through the clouds. "Look, Mommy," he said, "It's like God's shining a big flashlight down on us." At that age, he had a dream catcher on his wall and a pendulum on his bedside table. There was a porcelain angel who watched him from a bookshelf and a yin/yang necklace he wore around his neck. Faith is faith.

What Does God Look Like?

I was visiting photography professor at Harvard during the winter semester of 1998. One of my students sang in the choir in the chapel service held from 8:45 to 9:00 A.M. daily. Every morning, a member of the faculty, or someone connected to the University, gave a five-minute sermon, which was carefully structured into that fifteen-minute format. After attending each Tuesday and having expressed a desire to speak at some point, I got a call from the Chaplain's Office, assigning me a sermon at the end of that week.

I asked if I could talk about anything I wanted. I was reassured that, as Harvard faculty, I could. So I spoke about my photographs of healers, which were relatively new at the time. I talked about the strange effects I was getting on the film and I questioned whether these photographs would change my faith—or someone else's.

Standing at the podium of the Appleton Chapel at Harvard University, in a clerical gown, I felt more present in my body than at any other talk I'd ever given about my photography. I also felt I was being heard in a way that I never had been before.

One morning a few days later, I was lying in bed, awake but not ready to get up. Suddenly there appeared before me what I could only refer to as a vision. Somehow I knew to kneel before this huge, elderly man with a long, gray beard and a red-orange glowing robe. He was very big and I remember thinking before I looked up at him that I hoped it wasn't Jesus because I might not believe this was happening if it were. He wasn't recognizable to me, I noticed that his robe had radiant, iridescent transparency. He was impressive. He said quite clearly, "Your job is to help the healers heal." And being ill with immune deficiency problems, I replied, "Oh great, what about me?" And he said, "You are well." That was all. He was gone. I'd like to think I thanked him, but I'm not certain I did.

Even now, when I think back on these few moments, I realize how blessed I am to have had such a remarkable experience. Before this I had only known the existence of Spirit in the abstract. And now there was a messenger to confirm it. Yes—I had been heard at Harvard. There had been many that were listening. And I had even been given an assignment!

The big question in my mind, which had always

gone unanswered until just recently was, who was it exactly that had appeared to me some 6 years ago? Who was that guy in the red-orange robe that had given me my instructions? He is Swami Sri Yukteswar, known for his teachings that bridge the gaps between religions, and for his devotion to the many different ways of seeing. There is one published book of his teachings called *The Holy Science*, and the well-known book *Autobiography of a Yogi*, by Paramahamsa Yogananda was written about him. He lived in India from 1855 to 1936.

As a teacher of photography, one assignment I loved giving to my students was to make an image of what God or Spirit looked like to them. Like many of us who grew up rooted in the tradition of one faith or another, I saw God as an omnipotent deity. It was an image that was reinforced by my art education and especially by the "Creation of Adam," Michelangelo's painting on the ceiling of the Sistine Chapel that I had seen reproduced so many times (and that had been echoed by Steven Spielberg's image of E.T. and Elliot touching fingers).

In 1990, I utilized my patented technology to create an image called "Jesus/Mohammed/Buddha," a composite image of all three faces (The Mohammed image was derived from an etching I found in the photo archive of the New York Public Library.). After September 11, I re-titled this image "One" and used it in direct response to the event in the many Downtown art exhibits that followed. For me, this was always a piece that asked the viewer to consider what that God-concept looks like to them.

Returning to the same subject in 2000, I took out several ads in local newspapers for a series called "Guys Who Look Like Jesus." The ads read "Jesus look-alikes, all ethnicities wanted. Please send us your photo if you think you look like Jesus and want to be photographed." It was a project inspired by two friends of mine. One friend was sporting long hair and a beard and when someone commented that he looked like Jesus, he immediately cut it all off. My other friend, on the other hand, is a healer who loves looking like Jesus and actively chooses that look for himself.

I was curious to find out what inspires men to cultivate a "Jesus look" and I was not surprised to find that each person had a different reason for maintaining that look. Some of the "Guys" have a very intense spiritual life. One was conducting workshops dressed like Jesus. Another just had had a bad haircut in high school, and chose never to cut his hair again. Ultimately, I combined the "Guys" I photographed into one image, and juxtaposed it with an image I made by combining historical Jesus paintings.

The point I wanted to illustrate by showing the composites side-by-side was the discrepancy between our modern iconography of Jesus and the more Semitic version, which might in fact be more historically and genetically accurate. What Jesus looks like –or what God looks like—is a constantly morphing personal concept for each of us. As we grow older, our relationship to our image of God evolves into what constitutes our new image of God, one that is woven into the intricate multi-dimensional composites that are ourselves. Imagine, in the midst of a bad day, how much that image of our God can change. On a good day, whether we're feeling grateful or deeply in love, again that image shifts. The more aware we are of who we are, the more awareness we have of the changing face of God, the one that's reflected back in our own face.

A Lesson in Faith

A woman who has been the curator of a large museum in Texas has been a friend of mine since 1992

"One," a composite portrait of Jesus, Mohammed,
and Buddha

when she curated the first mini-retrospective and traveling exhibition (with accompanying book) of my work. Beside the natural bond that occurs between artist and curator, our friendship was well-rooted in the fact that our sons were born two weeks apart.

Over the years since that exhibition, my friend has been a frequent, always-welcome houseguest during her periodic art hunting trips to New York City. On one such visit last year, I awoke at 5:00 in the morning and heard her moving in and out of the bathroom several times. Then she called out to me that she was really sick and needed a doctor. I got up and found her throwing up on the bathroom floor, in intense pain. She told me the pain was more intense than giving birth. I didn't know what the problem was, but when I saw her color I called an ambulance. I kept thinking to myself, people are supposed to heal in my space, not get sick. There must be a reason why my friend is so sick that she can't get off the floor of my bathroom. I knew it wasn't life threatening, but I also couldn't figure out what was wrong. She was extremely frightened and began giving me instructions regarding her kids if she should die. I told her she wasn't going to die on my watch and as

I kept my hand running energy up her spine, I knew she would be okay.

A few hours later in the emergency room at St. Vincent's Hospital, she was diagnosed as having three kidney stones—one of them four millimeters large which had ripped her kidney. What is going on here? I wondered. Is this a lesson? What's "right" about this that I wasn't seeing?

Later that day—a Tuesday, I remember—my friend, heavily medicated, got on a plane and went back home. She was scheduled to have surgery three days later. On that Friday, she was hospitalized and anesthetized. To the surgeon's surprise, the kidney stones had disappeared and the rip in the kidney had completely healed.

When she told me all of this, I was stunned. A four-millimeter kidney stone—gone. What had happened? They had given her an ultra sound treatment to break up the stone, and perhaps it had worked. But what about the rip in the kidney that had been repaired, magically and completely? Certainly, I had prayed for her. And I had told a few other healers who had also sent prayers.

More importantly, I had not only prayed for my friend but I had focused my thoughts on her. I'd thought about our friendship and what seemed like our karmic connection. I had thought about my gratitude for her in my life. Did she really have a higher power? Did she really believe in Source? Was this a lesson for both of us in the power of prayer and positive thought? So when we spoke a few weeks later I said, "did you get it, did you get the lesson?" And she said she had. She had been given a lesson in faith and the power of prayer and it had been received.

Here's the bottom line: If you accept that focusing, or prayer, or positive thoughts are effective, whether you think it works because of a supreme being or simply energy, it doesn't matter. It all works! It doesn't matter who or what your focus is, as long as you focus. You can focus on specific outcomes or for the highest good of a specific event or individual. You can even simply focus on your breathing, because when you're focusing on your breath, you're still maintaining a focus. And you're connected to the God/Goddess consciousness that is the core essence of our being.

When I began photographing healers, I never expected that I would become one. Yet the success in curing cancer and other life-threatening illnesses that I have witnessed in the process of photographing one group of healers in particular, has lead to my involvement in promoting the acceptance of energy healing as an integral part of alternative medicine. I can say with pride that my work with the healers over the past few years has been responsible for the recovery of many people with cancer and other serious illnesses. After connecting one of my favorite craniofacial kids, Sammy (who is now in his mid-twenties) with one of the healers, Sammy's facial scarring, from over 50 surgeries, was dramatically reduced using energy. Most impressive is the fact that his nose is now one third less its original size. Harvard is now actively studying this healer's work.

There was one client that I worked on steadily for several years. He is a friend of my son's who came to me with a serious disease four years ago. After working on him for a year, his disease went into remission. He is my own personal success story.

THREE

Find Your Teachers

WHY DO WE NEED TEACHERS? WHEN WE STAND in the presence of those who are powerful, we capture their energy, or their frequency for knowing and doing what they do. Some teachings are "taught," and some are "caught," so whether we are going to church or going to a meditation, taking a yoga class, focusing on our breath, or reading a book like this one, we are literally catching the energy and frequency of whoever is guiding us. And we can use that energy from those teachers to boost our own awareness. It's why people see my aura so easily when I show them.

The most important thing to remember about finding your teachers is that they are only there to remind you what your higher self already knew. You are your own guru and a teacher is only right for you if they're allowing you to be and become who you really are. Take a class or a workshop. The more teachers you're exposed to, the more tools you accumulate in your tool box. You can learn a lot on the Internet, and there are books and web sites listed at the back of this book for that purpose.

No one person is right for everyone. For example, there is one spiritual counselor who comes to New York City periodically who I did not have a good experience in visiting. Yet everyone else in my community embraces him when he's in town. Their collective truth isn't my personal heartfelt truth. It was a good lesson for me that I'm entitled to my own opinion, and to trust that I know who I resonate with and whose energy makes me feel "less than." You also may not align and agree with 100 percent of what you're being taught—and you're entitled to disagree. A good teacher will understand that. The bottom line is if you ask to find teachers, they will come to you. You might even ask someone you admire how they know what they know.

My Teachers

When I first met Starr Fuentes, I photographed her. I'd never seen anyone emit so much energy, nor had I ever witnessed such an ability to manipulate it and seal it in other people's bodies. Starr controlled every shot, telling me the exact moment to press the shutter. I was fascinated and intimidated. I was also unaccustomed to taking so much energy into my body. I left the session feeling rather sick.

In the weeks and months that followed, I sat with Starr or walked beside her, accompanying her to various public events. I watched her and I photographed her again and again. I watched Starr watch other people and I observed firsthand her extraordinary psychic ability, as well as her capacity to transform disease. I also saw her take someone's cancer into her own body temporarily, in an effort to remove it completely. It's a process I've come to know as a profound demonstration of unconditional love.

Spending time with Starr was filled with extraordinary moments. I watched her spot a sick person fifty feet away, and simultaneously know the intimate details of that person's sex life. I listened as she calmly but firmly warned someone of impending death if they continued to be careless on a motorcycle or deal in drugs. I witnessed her heal people instantly of injuries which they had suffered from for decades.

The first time I was finally alone and face-to-face with Starr, we were sitting in a coffee shop across a table from each other. I was interviewing her, feeling a bit uncomfortable, asking her question after question. Having tuned into my anxiety at being alone with her for the first time, she said, "Nancy, we are going to know each other and be very close friends until the day I die . . . and that's not for a long time. So, breathe." The breath I inhaled at that moment marked the beginning of our friendship.

There is no doubt in my mind that Starr Fuentes is one of the best psychics and healers in the world today. She spent 15 years in the rain forests and deserts of the world, learning her craft from every *curandera*, witch doctor, or shaman that would allow her to study. She is the lineage-holder for the ancient Mayan traditions of healing, skills that she has only been allowed to teach for the past seven years. Her contribution to the world of healing is significant, surpassed only by her power to teach it to others. A lot of the knowledge I've compiled for this book, I learned from Starr.

Starr Fuentes had the most devastating childhood

of all the people I have ever met or known in my life. She was starved as a child, beaten by both parents, and sexually abused by her father. At the age of five, she found her sister's body hanging from a light fixture over her parent's bed. Her parents were still in that bed, too drunk to notice.

Starr had every intention of becoming a nuclear physicist, but during her senior year at Michigan State, there was a Mensa party (an organization whose members have high IQs in common) for one of the members who had a plum size cancerous tumor growing on his upper arm. He was scheduled for surgery the next day. As the party was ending, Starr cupped her hand over the tumor and the tumor came off in her hand. A single drop of blood dripped onto his arm. They both screamed and she threw the tumor up into the air. It hit the ceiling, fell onto a table, bounced off and rolled underneath. She ran from the room and never saw him again. Starr spent the next few days mourning that she would never be the nuclear physicist that she'd always hoped to be. It was predestined that healing was her path.

At the age of 65, I believe that Starr's life serves as a model for all those who have experienced physical or

Starr Fuentes. This photograph was taken at her retreat center, Casa Alma, near Houston, Texas

sexual abuse. She still devotes part of her time to healing the sexual abuse of others. She also conducts tantric workshops for couples, the result of the teachings she learned in the course of healing her own abuse at Tantra school in India.

Some teachers are in our lives for only a few hours. Father Zlatko Sudac is a 33-year-old Croatian priest who thousands of people gather to see wherever he appears. In 1998 he developed a Stigmata in the form of a cross on his forehead which still bleeds periodically. In 2000, he received the stigmata on his wrists, feet, and side. Father Sudac's marks were studied and tested in Rome for months and the conclusion of the investigation was that his phenomena are unexplainable. I went to see him at a church in Greenwich Village a few years ago. I stood in the cold for an hour-and-a-half because I could feel his energy outside the church, and it was unlike anything I'd ever felt before. Father Sudac spoke simply about the heart. He asked simple questions. "Many people think with their head but is your intellect everything? Do you think it's impossible to think with the heart? Do you think it's impossible to live with your heart?" And then he said, "open your heart." And when he said that, I immediately felt my heart open like a time-lapse photo of a flower unfolding. What an amazing feeling it was! I'd never experienced anything like that before.

By the time I met Gary Douglas, the founder of "Access," I had already taken some of his classes. "Access" is a powerful set of tools used to achieve consciousness, which Gary invented 15 years ago. It's a way of life, as well as a way of being.

One tool that I learned from Gary is to ask the question, "How does it get any better than this?" Try it. Asking this question is one of the fastest ways to lighten the energy of a situation. If you find yourself suddenly involved in a disagreement, or even if you're tired, out of sorts, or not feeling well, the best way to lighten the energy is to say (to yourself or out loud) "How does it get any better than this?" If you're in a situation in which you're feeling quite content and you want to feel even better, asking the same question still works. So if the energy is high, it will get even higher. Just keep asking, "How does it get any better" and it will.

"Who does this belong to?" is another Access tool, as well as "An interesting point of view."

There are about 2,000 people who use Access and

Gary Douglas. When this photograph was printed in color, an orange streak of light appeared over his heart. It is visible here in black and white as a lighter color and is what he calls his "doorway to Access."

a whole family of Access practitioners, which stretches across the globe from Australia and New Zealand to Europe and across the U.S. and Canada.

The day before a retrospective of my work at the Grey Art Gallery in New York City in 2002, Gary and I went to the museum for a quick preview of my exhibition. I made some introductions to the museum staff and installers as they finished the last-minute details before the opening. They all recognized him immediately from his photo, the one with the light coming out of his heart. Since Gary's presence tends to draw people toward him, he chatted with the staff as we moved together from room to room until we came to the largest space in the museum where Gary's photograph was hanging. He had never seen the 39″ x 39″ version before and it was a lot bigger than he anticipated. Or, at least that was what I thought he was reacting to when I felt his energy shift. He suddenly excused himself and went back to his hotel.

Less than a day later, Gary lay in intensive care in New York Hospital closer to death than life. They had removed the cysts that had blocked his airway in a life-threatening infection that was never diagnosed as bacterial or viral. While Gary lay in intensive care,

I spent the week blaming myself that somehow my picture had made him sick.

A week passed in which the global network of Access workers prayed for his recovery. I went to see him as soon as he was moved from the ICU. I said, "Gary, what happened? Did you really hate the picture?" He said the picture was important. "Of course it is" I said, "It's your energy that came through onto the film."

"That's only one reason why it's important. What I hadn't realized is that's the doorway to Access and consciousness right there over my heart. I knew when I saw it, that I hadn't opened the door all the way. I knew that once that door was unlocked, that time would unlock as well. Once that happens, the past, present, and future will coexist in the constant state of now. That way, we will all perceive, know, be, and receive with the clarity that we have so many choices, and that we can all function in greater consciousness."

Gary believes that we should take whatever feelings we have about a situation and make those feelings infinite. When we think of something as expanding to the size of the universe, if the concept itself is true and real, it expands. The concept of love, for instance, is infinitely expansive. If we take the concept of war and expand that, the energy dissipates and it becomes less substantial, dissolving completely.

Jodi Serota is another close friend of mine who is also a Master. She is a master of sound and the sounds that she makes are profoundly healing. Jodi was also instrumental in teaching me the language of consciousness and positive focus. It was after one of Jodi's classes several years ago that my own vision shifted dramatically, and I began to see the pathways of complicated intricate patterns in the dark over my head, which light up each of my nights. Jodi's class that evening had been about the value and importance of creating intention, and I had held an intention to broaden my vision. I still see the delicate webs before me over my bed each night. They illuminate my life in a way that has opened my own heart. They are different every time I see them and every time I see them I want to photograph them. Whether they are pathways to other dimensions, or a daily chronicle of morphogenetic forms created by the words and events of the day, they are still a reminder to me of the value of intention.

Jodi Serota, after a sound concert she gave at the United Nations in 2003

Derek O'Neill, the Irish psychotherapist and Reiki Grand Master, is another teacher of mine. If Derek gives one of his "The Truth Will Set You Free" workshops in your city, I recommend that you sit in his presence for the day (proceeds go to the children of India). What you will learn for yourself, you will keep in your heart your whole life.

Derek truly enables those present to make real changes for themselves. His energy is a blessing of limitless love for us all. He fills large spaces and hundreds of people with so much energy that you will leave with an energetic high that is the essence of pure love. I've seen him walk up and down aisles of people, looking for the person whose "higher self" was communicating to him that they would have a heart attack unless he healed it that day. He is also able to transform life-threatening tumors into benign cysts, saving many lives. Derek tells us that we must "start the day with love, spend the day with love, and end the day with love."

It is Derek's belief that prayers or focused intent should be written down. When we write down what we want, the awareness of the intent of each word helps draw our attention toward our intention. His Holiness Sri Sathya Sai Baba, Derek's mentor, (the

Derek O'Neill conducting a life-changing workshop in New York City in 2003.

Indian Avatar worshipped by millions there) had a vision of Derek addressing the UN (which he did last year), as well as the United States Congress. It is a vision I also believe will come to be.

FOUR

How Energy Works and How to Focus Yours

HOLD YOUR HANDS A FEW INCHES APART, PALMS facing each other. Do you "feel" something—a magnetism—between them? You might feel a warmth or a cool feeling or a tingling around your fingers. Everyone feels energy differently because each of us is unique, and we all have our own individual "frequency." For years now, one of the first things I do when people come to my studio is demonstrate what it's like to "feel energy" or chi. It's what George Lucas calls "the Force" and what Mel Brooks calls "the Schwartz."

Every time I've done an interview for TV and

someone has put a microphone on me, the microphone produces audible static. Everyone thinks that the microphone is broken, so they try another one, but the same thing happens! This is the point at which I explain that my frequency is quite magnetic and the microphone is picking it up.

There are several different ways of experiencing the energy around us. There are those who feel it and others who see it. The "see-ers" can actually see the aura of energy around people, as well as animals and objects. There are several levels of aura and some "see-ers" see the "personality" colors of people that appear around the body, while others see the physical health of people directly over the body. Other "see-ers" see the energetic connections between people which appear like cords of light between their bodies. Some people see energy only with their eyes closed. They use their closed eyes like a TV screen to "tune in." To experiment, close your eyes for a few minutes and focus on the "screen" in front of you. You might see more than you think!

How do you know whether you're predominately a see-er, hearer, or feeler of energy? A visionary sees pictures, the auditory hears sounds, and feelers feel their feelings. Here's a way to tell in which modality your brain prefers to store information. To find out which modality you are, ask yourself a question about your past, something like: What did I do on my last birthday? Notice that your eyes move slightly to search for the memory of the event. Eyes that move upward which search to see the picture in their minds are visionaries. Eyes that move from side to side (ear to ear) search for sounds and are auditory. Eyes that move down toward the heart are feelers.

Visual people see in pictures and have difficulty remembering verbal sequences. They use phrases like "see you," "watch it," "I notice," "it appears," "it looks like." Auditory people are attentive to speech. They remember verbal sequences easily and learn by listening. They use words or phrases like "listen," "that sounds like," "I hear," "it's good to talk," "that rings true." If you're an auditory person then what you hear is the most important of the senses to you. You're liable to react if something doesn't sound true for you. Kinesthetic people rely on their "gut feelings" and on their sense of touch for what they're doing. Touching things captures their attention. They use phrases like "I feel like," "I can handle," "hold on," "get in touch." If you're a feeler, your expectations won't be met if something is not passionate enough for you.

If you're a visually-oriented person, then you're liable to get frustrated or angry when something or someone ruins your picture. If you're an auditory person, then what you hear from people is the most important thing to you. You might react if something doesn't sound true to you. If you're a feeler, you're likely to be able to feel a little prickly bristle-like magnetism around your body and especially around your head. "Feelers" can even tell the difference between what is the truth and what is a lie by measuring the energy of each. What is right is light and it literally feels lighter.

Words vibrate! Some years ago, some researchers in Japan discovered that by labeling vials of water with different messages, such as "Love/Appreciation" versus "You Make Me Sick," you could actually see the effect of each translated in the water crystals themselves. The "Love/Appreciation" crystal appeared like a diamond-like snowflake, while the "You Make Me Sick" crystal distorted, imploding into asymmetrical shapes.

In 2000, I collaborated with the Russian physicist Dr. Konstantin Korotkov in producing images with his newest invention, the GDV, or Gas Discharge Visualization camera. Popular in Russia and Eastern

Europe, this camera records energy fields or auras. The images themselves are aural fingerprints which incorporate digital Kirilian photography with computer analysis in mapping and evaluating an individual's state of health.

With the help of Dr. Korotkov and his GDV camera, I was able to capture images that clearly showed the differences between positive and negative thought, and between anger and love. These aural images were made with the help of the healers, Jodi

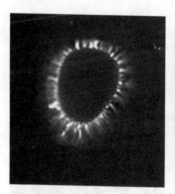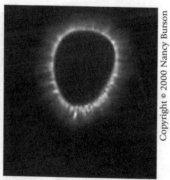

The differences between negative thought (photo on left) and positive thought (photo on right). These "aural fingerprints" were taken with a GDV (Gas Discharge Visualization) camera in collaboration with Jodi Serota, who manipulated her thoughts and emotions through sound.

Serota and Starr Fuentes, who attained a range of emotional states in order to generate the images.

Look at the differences between the positive and negative thoughts that are reproduced here in these photographs. Negative thoughts appear choppy, without the same flow that positive thoughts have. The differences between positive messages and negative messages resonate completely differently in your physical body!

 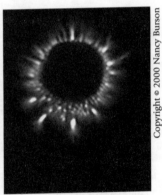

The differences between anger (photo on left) and love (photo on right). These photos were taken with a GDV (Gas Discharge Visualization) camera in collaboration with Starr Fuentes.

Now look at the differences between anger and love. Anger appears one sided and unbalanced, whereas love appears like a beautiful diamond necklace.

Try an experiment. Say out loud, "I love you." You can focus on a certain person when you do this. Then say, "I hate you." You can keep someone in mind if you want, but if you do, apologize to that person after you do this. And if you use yourself as an example, be sure to apologize to yourself! Sense how powerful these words are and how you respond to the differences between them. If you're a "see-er," you'll visualize love and hate as images in your mind. An auditory person will measure the differences in terms of their frequency and which sounds lighter. "Feelers" will feel the difference between them.

When I do demonstrations of energy and someone doesn't see my aura, the chances are they might be a "feeler" or a "knower." A "knower" just knows what a given energy is. They cannot explain how they know, but they just do. They have "knowing." After a lecture recently, a student came up to me and said, "I know now that I am a 'knower.' I've never known what to call that sense that I have, but you're right, I'm a 'knower!'" He was thrilled to have an explanation for the way he knows things.

It really doesn't matter how we know what we know. What matters is that we do know, and that we acknowledge that we know. We each have our own power, our own wisdom, and our own self-awareness. Derek O'Neill talks about L-I-F-E, an acronym for "Look Inside For Everything."

We are all-knowing. Knowledge is power and knowing is empowering. We don't need to say, "I don't know." All we need to do is to focus and ask to know. All the answers to all the questions lie within each of us. We have everything we need. And when we discover who we are, it enables us to stay in our power. We are all Masters and each of us holds God or Spirit within us. We are all a part of that energy, and so is the guy walking besides us. Let's all treat each other just like that. And let's all speak to each other as the Gods and Goddesses that we are . . . and treat our children and mates the same way. Let's parent our children as if a lot of people we respect are watching us.

There are people who receive audio and hear actual messages that come through one's higher self, which I believe guides us all. Sometimes that guidance can come through one's own voice and sometimes people hear different voices inside their heads.

There are even people who have a combination of all these abilities to detect energy and can access each with ease. Usually these people are those who are experienced at focusing, praying, or meditating and who have a regular daily spiritual practice.

Picture this: you're having a good day. For whatever reason, you feel really optimistic and happy. And then you walk into a room and the people there, whether it is a boardroom, classroom, or family room, have had a "down" or bad day. Suddenly you realize that you're in a terrible mood. You can't explain why, but that great optimism you just had has been replaced by negativity, leaving you feeling drained and tired.

What happened? You got zapped with other people's energy. When you walked in, you were the highest, lightest person in the room. Unfortunately, everyone else needed what you had and, without being at all aware of it, they took your energy. Energy runs from the highest source to the lowest source. It's totally natural and it's how energy works.

Notice who you love to be around and who is needy and harder to be around. Love is a frequency and need is a much lower vibration. Love brings energy to you and need pulls energy away. Remember that we cannot make others happy. They have to do their own homework to get that, and you cannot do it for them. It is self-love that so powerfully effects how we love others. We cannot unconditionally love our mates, our children, or our friends, without enough self-love to sustain it. Indeed, one cannot give the gift of love to those unwilling to receive it.

You can stand beside people and support them lovingly, but ultimately we are each responsible for our own personal growth and self-awareness. Spirit doesn't require us to heal others at the expense of ourselves. When you are the easiest person to get along with, in your family, at school, at work, or in relationships, chances are you're taking on a lot of the energy of others. You're the person others seek advice from or who is called to mediate conflicts. This is because you are the healer and the "empath." And you are the best and highest source of energy.

When we are acting as empaths and taking on other people's energy, one good thing to remember is to ask ourselves "Who does this belong to?" The chances are, it's not ours. If we ask this question, the energy around us will shift and lighten because we have probably taken on something that doesn't belong to us, and we are far better off letting go of what isn't ours. It's the easiest and fastest way to get rid of a headache or stomachache that we suddenly acquire. For instance, "Who does that cold belong to?" If it's not yours, don't take it on! Try asking the question and you will see that if something doesn't belong to you, it leaves quickly. A lot of what we grew up with isn't ours. It originally belonged to our parents. If you're reacting to something or someone, it may be left over from your childhood, and if you ask who it belongs to, you can become aware of the source of the reaction you're having.

"What you resist, persists" is another way in which energy works. I believe we are all here to learn certain lessons and that we will be given those lessons again until we learn them. If for instance we're afraid of being abandoned, then chances are we will create that pattern for ourselves until we are conscious and aware enough to change it. Then we can live our lives with real abandon, knowing that the only person who will never abandon us is ourselves.

People who are fearful are given more to fear. Those who are loving get more love. We create what we most fear. When we're aware of the problems that we are creating, we can shift them. I recently met a mother who was upset that her eight-year-old son had a cavity in every tooth. She told me she had had very bad teeth all her life. Her concern for her son was so great that she had brushed her son's teeth herself until he was six. What this woman did not realize is that her worry was actually a prayer for something she didn't want. What she resisted persisted. What she feared the most was given to her.

How many times a day do we say or think to ourselves, "that's right," or "so and so is wrong about that." How often do we tell ourselves "this person is . . ." or—you fill in the blanks. All of these statements are judgments. Having them is human. But what if our response is simply, "that's an interesting point of view." Then we would have no judgments and we could just be in gratitude. When we speak to others without judgment, every conversation becomes an opportunity for growth. The less we judge, the more we can forgive. The fewer judgments we make, the more choices we create.

There are so many choices we allow ourselves when we are not constantly judging others. The amount of energy we spend blessing situations or people is so much more positive than that which we expend in negative energy by judging them. There are three reasons why we make judgments: value, power, and safety. Does this person make us feel valueless, powerless, or unsafe? The next time you are walking down the street, or are in an environment where there are a lot of people, analyze for yourself what the reason is for your judgment. There is some MIT research that indicates that we decide in the first 3–5 seconds whether or not we like someone based solely on their appearance. If there is someone that you immediately don't like, ask yourself whether they make you feel valueless, powerless, or unsafe. Chances are if you were physically abused in any way, issues of safety will be significant to you. When I first began to do this work, I was shocked at how often I was in judgment of people passing by me on the street. Once we become aware of the number of judgments we have against people that we don't even know, we can begin to change that pattern and create a different intention. If you have a judgment against someone, the best thing to do is to bless them. By blessing them, you cancel the judgment against them. After all, in terms of the bigger picture, what feels lighter to us, being right or being happy?

It is important to bless those whose opinions differ from ours. This will feel so much better than judging them because their thoughts are different than ours. We are all right!

What We Think Can Change the World

If we take a few minutes a day to focus, pray, meditate, or visualize, we can shift the collective conscious with our thoughts. It does work, and Quantum Physics has proved it. If we each took five minutes a day to focus, what we give by saying prayers for others, we get back in the form of love of self and self-realization. We feel a lot more content with ourselves and our relationships and we bring ourselves closer to the things we really want.

If we look at energy as one aspect of God, then everything is a part of God. In fact, one friend of mine thinks of GOD as an acronym for "Get Over Defining!" Energy follows thought, so the more positive our thoughts are, the more positive charge there is on the energy to support us.

Psychologists tell us that we each think between 65,000 to 70,000 thoughts per day and that 90 to 95% of them are repetitive.

When we think negatively, our lives will be reflected

in the same way. Metaphysical authority and host of the popular cable show, New Realities, Alan Steinfeld says, "We are not our minds, we just think we are. Our minds are so distracting. Let's not listen to them." Each of us creates our own reality and what we think can change the world. Every thought is a prayer and worry is a prayer for something we don't want. Don't ever think your thoughts are private. Every one of them is heard by the thought police in the ether that is God, or Oneness, or Spirit, or Consciousness.

When we focus, we hold the potential to assist ourselves and others energetically. When we think positively about someone, it's the same as a prayer. If you're sending negative thoughts, you're putting out prayers of negativity, which will place you in "victim" mode. By simply realizing your thoughts are negative, you are on your way to turning around your incoming messages to something positive It's already a form of conscious awareness that you can shift and change negative thoughts. When we know how to focus, we can access our power. We can access the keys to empowerment by learning how to ask for exactly what we want.

For some, one possible immediate consequence to

an increase in awareness might mean temporary changes in our physical or emotional selves. These are shifts that test our relationships to ourselves and to those around us. They can cause us to question every aspect of our being. Starr Fuentes says, "It's what happens when you put light into a vessel. What isn't light (pure) raises to the surface." In that case, it's up to us not to judge ourselves or our reactions. The more compassion we give ourselves in those moments of confusion, the more we are able to open again to new opportunities and new wisdom. Confusion is fusion. It breaks our boundaries and moves us toward enlightenment. So if you're confused, take a breath and know that "shift happens" (or "what the shift")!

The most effective way to focus is one-to-one. One prayer or one visualization for others entitles you to ask for one thing for yourself. This is the best way to manifest what you want and it's an effective source of positive thought. For example, if you're asking for safety for your family, you might also ask that your friends' families and members of your community be safe as well. If you're asking for inner peace, then you might also ask for peace within your family unit or peace between nations. Decide what you want to ask for and ask for exactly that. It doesn't matter whether you ask for God's help, or Buddha's, or Allah's. You can ask the Universe for help, or Holy Spirit, or the Divine mother, or Oneness. All you have to do is keep asking. Be clear, be simple, and be specific. No begging!

Keep your focus and prayers positive. Prayers using the word "no," negatives, and "don'ts" consume your energy pushing AGAINST something. For instance, there is no way to "fight" for peace. We must live peace, think peace, and be peaceful in order to create peace. We must receive peace, and surrender in peace. If we add our anger toward war, what we create is the energy to feed more war. Feelings of safety and security come from within us. Therefore we can create and amplify a lasting peace within ourselves.

We can focus on sending love to all our leaders whether or not we agree with them. We can surround our leadership with love and light and bless them instead of allowing ourselves to be controlled by our anger, fear, or frustration at our world right now. Let us send the energy of the love in our hearts out to the leaders of our country and to all the world leaders whose countries are in conflict now.

In order to augment the energy of thoughts or

prayers, pray with something. This increases the amount of energy moving toward your intention. For example, let's ask that the number of people wanting lasting peace in the Middle East be doubled (every three weeks). Or, "Let each breath I take add to the energy of peace within myself and throughout the world." When I focus, I use: "I ask that . . ." or "I request that . . ." on a regular basis. "Please deliver" or "bring this to me" works too.

Even if you develop a simple practice of 5 minutes of focus daily, you and the rest of the world will benefit.

Focusing or saying prayers requires practice just like every other skill we acquire. The more time you put into spiritual practice the more effective you will be, and the more benefit you'll derive from it. It's simple: The more you give, the more you get back. If you're in one of the service professions, such as teaching, nursing, or policing, your occupation is already a signal to Source that you have committed the bulk of your energy in giving to others. So know that you are entitled to have what you want, too.

Quality prayers require that we turn off the phone and are fully present. Even if we only have a few minutes to focus, commit fully to those quality minutes without distraction from children or television.

When groups of people pray together, the power of that agreement amplifies those prayers. Groups of people who pray together don't necessarily have to be in the same place at the same time. They simply need to be in agreement to pray for the same results.

On Sunday, September 14, 2003, Hurricane Isabel was reported to be a Category 4 storm moving across the open ocean with winds clocked at 160 miles per hour. On that Sunday, with the winds at that speed—nearly as powerful as a hurricane can get—federal forecasters said that "only minor fluctuations in intensity are expected for the next couple of days." However, on September 18, the *New York Times* reported that the intensity of the hurricane had proved unpredictable; by Tuesday, its winds had dropped by 50 m.p.h. the *Times* reported on September 20 that "for all the apocalyptic forecasting, Hurricane Isabel moved through the New York region with more of a whimper than a bang. High winds pushed over trees and pulled down power lines, but the fears of extensive flooding that prompted officials to declare emergencies and muster rescue vehicles proved groundless."

On Monday, September 15, I knew that Hurricane

Isabel would not hit the New York area directly and that it would moderate in its intensity. There were hundreds of people who, like myself, were turning the energy of the storm backward with a clear intention and focus to slow it down. And although there is currently no real scientific proof, in my mind it remains a fine example of what groups of people can do to shift the energy of a situation when given the opportunity.

This is not to say that there wasn't a great deal of disaster due to Hurricane Isabel. However, if it had hit land at its peak speed, there would have been considerably more damage and more lives lost than there were.

The Un-vocabulary

Be exact in the words you choose, because exactly what you say is what you'll get. Eliminate the words that don't work. Here are some words to avoid.

• HATE. Hate is the opposite of love. Anything you hate you'll be given more of.

• WORRY. If this is what you're doing, you'll be given more to worry about. Remember that worry is a prayer for something you don't want in the future. Alternative: "I'm concerned that . . ."

• BUT. The only one you want in your life is the one you sit upon. If you use the word "but," you negate everything you said prior to that. An alternative is to use the word "and." If someone says to me for instance, "I may come, but I'm not sure if I can make it," I know that since the "but" was added, it's not going to happen.

• TRY. Trying is the attempt without succeeding. Watch how often you use this and eliminate it from your vocabulary. Use "allow" instead.

• NEED. Using the word "need" makes us feel that we are not enough, not whole. We are complete the way we are.

• WANT means to lack. All that we need or want, we already have within us, and we can ask to access that.

• NEVER doesn't exist. "Sometimes" works a lot better.

• SHOULD is a judgment. It implies that there is

some larger rule book that exists that tells you what you should and should not do. There is no rule book and people usually resent it when you tell them what to do. Ask people . . . "have you thought about? . . .

• ALWAYS is another global word like "never." Again, "sometimes" works better.

• WISH. If you're wishing for something, then you're not receiving. Instead of wishing, you could say: "It will be great when . . ."

• BLAME and FAULT. Blame and fault are huge judgments that don't work for anyone. Let's uncreate both of these, since nothing positive can come from either one. Ask instead . . . What can we learn from this disagreement? How can we interact better next time? How can we move on from here?

• BE CAREFUL. If this is what we're saying to our children, or anyone in our lives for that matter, it is a warning that makes the world seem even more dangerous (especially to a child). If this is the message we're giving to our children, we're really scaring them. Say instead "Be safe." it's a blessing, not a warning.

• I'M TIRED/I'M SICK. These statements will manifest as more of the same. Instead, fake it till you make it. Make statements like "I have lots of energy today" and "I feel great!"

Here are some positive words to use as often as possible.

• LOVE! Use this word more, and you will have more of it in your life.

• TRUTH! Whatever that is for you, stay in it.

• BEAUTIFUL! You are, and so is everyone else.

• ENJOYMENT! Being in joy!

• ENLIGHTENMENT! Being in light!

• BE-ING! The better alternative to do-ing, which can be do-do!

If you find yourself using these words or having negative thoughts, just cancel them. They're a part of being human and we all use them from time to time. Don't ever put yourself down. Every time you refer to yourself, or every time you say "I am," make sure what you say is positive.

When we talk about being responsible what we're really talking about is RESPOND-ABILITY, or the ability to respond to a given situation. How we respond is the key to being truly responsible.

Be Conscious
Consciousness is choosing to be responsible for every thought, word, and action that we take. When you realize you've said something that was negative or judgmental, just cancel those thoughts simply by saying, "I cancel that." Then say whatever it was over again in a more positive way. After we swear, "unswearing" is good to do too.

Take the time to express kindness and generosity to others and your kindness and generosity will be rewarded. The more time we take in focused prayer or thoughts, the more synchronistic our lives become. You'll think of someone and you'll suddenly hear from them. Or you'll think about something you want or need and then, like magic, it comes to you. All that we want comes to us and our lives are in flow. And let's not forget to focus on gratitude for all that we're receiving.

Always ask for "the highest good." For instance, if you're focusing on an elderly person to be healed of a certain disease, ask for that person's highest good. Then you're letting Source or Spirit decide what is best for that person. Some things aren't meant to be changed and those judgments belong only to Spirit.

You can also use "And so it is," which is another way of asking for the highest good. It is also a way of letting go of the outcome. There is a recent study suggesting that undirected prayers are even more effective than directed prayers, or those for a specific outcome. So when we are directing prayers for something or someone specifically, it's good to add, "and so it is," or "for the best and highest possible outcome." The study serves as a reminder that ultimately, we all need to let go and let whatever will be, be. Whether you believe in free will, Divine will, karma, all three, or none is insignificant. Does it really matter what the process is of how, who, or what is deciding? We can be specific in our focus and then let go of the outcome. Like the Beatles song "Let It Be," and so it is.

Be specific in your request. If you are asking for money, don't ask for abundance, ask for cash. Asking for abundance isn't specific enough. Neither is asking for money, because there are so many ways that can be interpreted as well. Focus on the fact that you already have it and it will come to you. And know that you deserve it! If you are worried about money and you are concerned about your bills, be careful what you are asking for. If you're saying to yourself, "Oh, I have so many bills!" that you'll end up with more bills, because that is what the universe is hearing you say you want. Remember that complaints only manifest more to complain about.

Recently I heard someone say, "I have so little love in my life." If that's what you've been saying, then that's what you will have. If you want love, come from a place that indicates that you already have it. Choose statements like "I am open to receive love," or "I am willing to be loved and nurtured." If it's a relationship you're looking for, then say, "I am in a loving relationship with . . ." and be specific about what you want in a mate. Whatever you tell yourself about relationships is what you will manifest for yourself. Relationships that end are a great opportunity to practice for the next one, which may be for a lifetime.

You can incorporate the lessons you learned in the last relationship and manifest exactly what's most important to you in the next. That means that it's time to rid ourselves of all that excess baggage and forgive our mate, partner, ex-husband, sibling, parent, or self. Marianne Williamson says "Forgiveness remains the only path that leads out of hell. Whether we're forgiving our parents, someone else, or ourselves, the laws of mind remain the same: As we love, we shall be released from pain, and as we deny love, we shall remain in pain." And Joan Borysenko says, "Forgiveness is the finishing of old business that allows us to experience the present, free of contamination from the past."

Everything in our lives is simply a reflection of who we truly are. Our relationship to ourselves is the same as our relationship to all the people in our lives. Our relationship to ourselves is the same as our relationship to our work, our talent, and our abilities. Our relationship to ourselves is the same as our relationship to our physical bodies and our sexuality. Our relationship to ourselves is the same as our relationship to our home, our environment, and the amount of organized space in our closets and drawers. Our relationship to ourselves is the same as our relationship to our money and finances. Our relationship to God, Source, and Spirit, governs our relationships to all the details of our lives. And lastly, our relationship to ourselves is equal to our relationship to God, Source, and Spirit.

Recently, someone said to me that he thought that the whole idea behind meditation was to rid yourself of your emotions. In fact, it's just the opposite. We learn a lot from our tears and our anger. When we allow ourselves our emotions, we learn to experience them fully without judgment. When we bury our emotions, they can manifest physically in our bodies. Most of us are angry or resentful about something or someone and we can use that angry space to control others. Those feelings occupy areas of our hearts that could be holding pure love instead. Now is the time. If we cannot forgive ourselves or others, we can find a therapist or healer to help resolve those issues, to enable us to move forward in our lives.

Once we've identified what our defining moments, or issues are, we can cut them away energetically using some simple techniques. As Starr says, "Own it and you can heal it!"

Getting Ready to Focus

One thing I like to do when I sit down to focus is to connect myself to Spirit with light. How do we see and feel light? We can visualize light as the brightest sunlight pouring into us. We can see ouselves connected to a huge light bulb. Remember that "beam me up" column of light from *Star Trek* that the Enterprise crew used to transport themselves? Most people have a pencil-thin connection to Source or God above their heads. We can increase that narrow tube of light to something much wider. We can have a highway of light coming into us, if that is what we choose.

What I focus on is a column of the brightest white light I can imagine, as far up in the sky as I can imagine it. I connect the column of light down through the top of my head all the way through my body and down into the earth as deeply as I can picture it. Then I'm connected. At this point, I feel light coming into me more profoundly if I take a few deep breaths and blow them out. Then I focus on extending the beam of light into a huge funnel coming into my head. If you do this sitting down, make sure you remember to uncross your legs and arms so that you're truly open to receiving. Flow with the glow.

You can also put light/energy down through you on the inhale breath, hold your breath for an instant at your heart and exhale it down into the earth. Then inhale up from the earth, hold your breath for an instant at your heart, and then exhale the breath upwards towards the sky. Then keep repeating this.

If you are feeling particularly angry or resentful,

breathe it out. Breathe in light and love at your heart, and breathe out all the anger and resentment and frustration that you feel.

Are you ready to really move on in your life and release all that anger and pain so you can live fully in the present? (It's a gift, that's why they call it "the present!") If you are truly ready to leave a person, relationship, or issue behind you and move into forgiveness, there are a few simple methods that will help you.

Put yourself in a quiet place and state of mind. You may want to run a lot of light through yourself before you begin to do this. Visualize the person you're letting go of sitting or standing in front of you. Visually, the two of you are connected by fibers. These fibers that link you may appear connected to many parts of your body and theirs. If you've been intimate with this person, there are energetic fibers that connect your sex organs. Imagine that you can call these fibers and have them come back to you. Then imagine the other person can have their fibers back as well. As you inhale, visualize all your fibers coming back to you and as you exhale, send their fibers back to them. You might want to remove these fibers systematically from each part of their body and yours. Continue this until you feel that that you have dissolved all the issues that were holding you together. It may take you a week of doing this off and on to feel the difference, but it will feel very different between you when you've finished.

Another method that clears issues from people is to picture yourself in a circle of gold light. Picture the issue or person in another circle of gold light right in front of you. Visualize your own sword of truth, your personal Excalibur, which only you can access for your own empowerment. If you like, you can picture it as a light saber similar to those used in "Star Wars." Using your own personal sword, draw a figure eight with brilliant blue light between you and whatever issue or person is in the circle of gold light in front of you. Do this until you feel that the issue or relationship has been dissolved.

If you're feeling "ungrounded," or not fully present in your body after you focus, it's a good idea to pull energy down through your feet and into the earth. Feel the support of Mother Earth at your feet. Another method of grounding is to stand up and turn your body completely around clockwise one rotation, then counterclockwise one rotation. It doesn't matter which way you turn first. The act of turning ourselves around helps us to remember our connection to the earth.

When I show people how to see my aura, I ask them to stand directly in front of me about ten or twelve feet away. Find a partner to do this. You can either stand or sit as long as you're both matching each other. The person whose aura is being looked at (the viewee) should be standing or sitting upright with their palms facing upwards. If the viewer is wearing glasses, it's best to remove them, as this is a natural way to de-focus your eyes. Focus your attention on the forehead of the person you're looking at. Concentrate on the area on the middle of the forehead between the eyes, often referred to as the third eye. De-focus your eyes (kind of like squinting a bit) and hold your attention on that spot only. When you keep your eyes focused on that spot, a rim of white light will begin to appear around the person in front of you.

Note: Ideal lighting conditions are anything but direct sunlight. Fairly dim light or daylight is fine, and it's fine if there's a light on in the room. It helps if the person you're looking at is wearing dark clothing on their upper body. A white or light wall works just as well as a darker wall. Remember that the aura is light. If you and your partner are standing there focusing on the other's third eye and you haven't seen anything yet, the two of you can take a few deep breaths and connect yourself to a column of the brightest white light you can think of, as high up in the sky as you can imagine, running all the way through your bodies and down deeply into the earth. Now the viewee can make their aura appear bigger if you take a few more deep breaths and continue to focus on bringing as much of the brightest light you can think of down through you. Then picture this light filling the entire room. This isn't difficult to do, but like other skills it takes a little practice. You can practice by yourself in your own bathroom mirror.

A few months after 9/11, a friend of mine got into an elevator with a man and woman who were in the middle of an intense dialogue. What he overheard was "I don't know what I want to do now," and the other agreed. There was a pause. And then, "I just want to see God" she said, and he agreed. These people had just lost their fiancés on Sept. 11. And in their loss they had expressed clearly the desire we all have to connect to more significant meaning in our lives. When I show people how to see my aura or feel energy, it's the clos-

In this photograph, taken at a lecture during my traveling retrospective exhitition, "Seeing and Believing," at Photo Espana in Madrid, 2003, I am showing the audience how to feel energy.

est way I have of showing others how to perceive God, Source, Spirit. It is my way of aligning us to our true God/Goddess selves. And it is my joy.

Find a partner and see if you can feel the energy between you. Hold your hands six to eight inches from theirs, or put their hands between both of yours.

It might be a tingle, cold, or warmth that you feel. Reverend Betsee Parker, the head chaplain at Ground Zero who was responsible for blessing the body parts at the site, told me she began to hear the weeping of God there. Dr. Parker describes the sound as similar to an Australian didgeridoo or Japanese Kota. When she finally decided to mention this to a colleague at the site, her fellow worker agreed that she'd also heard God weeping. When I am outside New York City, I often hear the sound, the frequency, of the earth. It can be very loud and it sounds like a steady low metallic hum, kind of like there's some very large appliance on. It's lower pitched in England and Scotland, and higher in Upstate New York. In Sedona Arizona, where there is a wide range in landscape, the sound shifts, and is sometimes higher, then lower again. I rarely hear this in New York City (except if there's a blackout), and when I do, it sounds very far away. When we become more experienced at tuning in, all our intuition opens, and we can access all the modalities of seeing, hearing, feeling, and knowing.

In the summer of 2002, Michael J. Berz and I went with a few friends to Jodi's country home a few hours from the city. Michael had just taken his brand new camera out of the box, and the first shots he took of my son had several large orbs, or light balls, in them. In fact, they were a stunning shock to all of us.

What are the orbs? Certainly they are a form of energy. John Burke, a geophysical researcher who's been gathering data that measures the earth's electromagnetic energies in the "sacred sites," (like Stonehenge and the pyramids of Egypt) says that at least some orbs are a form of plasma energy similar to lightning. They are, in a sense, electrified air.

All matter consists of solids, liquids, gases, and plasma (like lightning and the aurora borealis. According to John Burke, "when scientists create plasma energy in the laboratory, it self-organizes into circles and other shapes. Hexagons and triangles have also appeared in excited liquids, and plasma physics is essentially the physics of fluids (called magnetohydrodynamics)."

Our day in the country became even more memorable when Michael took a series of shots of Jodi, Alan Steinfeld, and me intending energy in the woods. It was in one of those shots that a yellow ball of light appeared in the middle of us, seemingly moving toward Jodi's hands. It had appeared for less than a second, and was gone in the next frame.

Michael J. Berz took this series of photos of Alan Steinfeld (here on the left), Jodi Serota (center), and me (right) in a circle while Jodi brought in energy through sound. In the fifth frame, a yellow sphere of energy appeared and was gone in the next frame, taken a split second later.

3

4

5

6

In the months that have followed, I've taken lots of pictures of orbs, and Michael and I have done many experiments to prove to ourselves and others that the orb phenomenon is real. When I shoot orbs, they appear round or hexagonal on my images. If Michael and I are standing next to each other and we shoot the same orb in the same position with different cameras, chances are that it's not dust! In fact, we've recently seen videotapes of them in motion, shot with an infrared camera.

Try shooting the orbs. Take your camera outdoors at night and see what you get. Use a camera that's either a digital or regular 35mm. (I prefer a digital.) Shoot with a flash, since light attracts light. Take a lot of pictures, not just one or two. Shoot a few rolls of film, or fill up a disk. Make an intention to shoot the orbs and you'll get them. The better you are at focusing or intending them, the more proficient you'll be at catching them on film.

You're most likely to find orbs in sacred sites, in and around houses of worship and cemeteries. There are some people who believe the orbs are dead people. My belief is that they tend to congregate where there is more electromagnetism in the earth and/or where there is unified thought. It's easier to capture them at night, but you can shoot them in daylight as well.

What We Can Do to Change the World

There are so many ways that we can envision a peaceful world. We can start by blessing all our enemies. We can ask that all terrorists shift their thinking. We can send magnetic energy to all nuclear weapons for disarming them. We can focus on dissolving the radiation of each nuclear weapon. We can envision embracing each and every terrorist. We can focus on enveloping the planet with white or gold light that penetrates each of us and penetrates deeply into the earth.

We can hold an image of an immense circle of humans holding hands, covering the entire circumference of the earth. Whatever way we choose to envision peace in the world is our own personal creation. It all works as effective prayer.

Whatever way you choose to focus works for one's inner peace as well. There are so many methods to choose from and different ways to visualize, meditate, or even chant. Whether it's focusing on your breath, or on repeating a particular word or sound, if it feels light, it's right for you.

Picture yourself as the connector between heaven and earth. Pull the energy of the earth's core up through your body, filling and saturating every cell. Then breathe into yourself the energy from the universe above. Allow both energies to meet at your heart. Remember, we heal others when we heal ourselves. Because we are all connected, when one of us shifts, we all do.

How do each of us connect to our hearts? How do we stop thinking with our heads and move instead into feeling from our hearts? And most importantly, how do we incorporate this shift into our lives? This is how easy it is. It doesn't matter whether you conceive of love emanating from your heart like a flowing white river of light, or a bouquet of flowers that you send, or valentine-shaped hearts. It doesn't matter what you conceive love to look like. What matters is that whatever symbolizes pure love to you, and that you'd like to be nurtured by yourself is the best way of sending love to others.

Breathe love and light in and out of your heart. Send it coming and going with each breath. The intention that you make is what directs the energy. Remember that what we think is just as important as what we say. So when we visualize or imagine what we want, it's just as powerful as saying it out loud.

Those who feel energy might conceive love as a warm tingle flowing in and out from their hearts. The "see-ers," or those that are more visual, tend to see love in some symbolic form or color, such as pink light. There is even a crystal bowl in the key of F that when activated, seems to create a pathway for connecting to our hearts through sound.

Focus on Peace

In late 1998, I was asked to do a commission for the London Millennium Dome, Britain's well-meaning, futuristic, but bizarre homage to the turning of the twenty-first century. Four football fields in size, the dome sat on the banks of the Thames River for the 12 months of the year 2000. With estimates that it would attract 10,000 visitors a day, it seemed a suitable place to introduce the newest of my (along with my collaborator, David Kramlich) interactive installations, The Human Race Machine. And even though estimates of the crowd didn't meet England's expectations, the Millennium Dome certainly drew far more people than the average art museum, the usual setting for my work.

Granted that there was more to see than to do in the

In 2000, Creative Time sponsored this billboard located at Church and Canal Streets in New York City with five images from The Human Race Machine which said "There's No Gene For Race."

Millennium Dome, visitors sometimes waited an hour-and-a-half in line to use The Human Race Machine, which shows viewers how they'll look as a different race. It was a great opportunity for people to step into another's shoes, and move conceptually from I-ness to We-ness. By using The Human Race Machine, viewers could move through difference and diversity to sameness. The more we recognize ourselves in others, the easier it is to connect the human race.

The first time The Human Race Machine was shown in New York City, in September 2000, it was accompanied by a billboard 20 x 60 feet high at the corner of Church and Canal Streets that read: "There's No Gene For Race." The billboard consisted of text accompanied by photos of the same person as five different races. (After Sept.11, the database was updated to include a Middle Eastern face.) The project was sponsored by Creative Time, an organization that has been presenting public art projects in New York City for the past 30 years, under the direction of the visionary Anne Pasternak for the past 8 years.

What a gratifying feeling and experience it was to hang out by the post office across from the billboard and eavesdrop on passers-by as they responded to the billboard. The Human Race Machine was my prayer for racial justice and the billboard felt like a vortex of positive thought promoting Oneness. How lucky I felt to have the kind of career that afforded me such amazing opportunities.

Nine months after September 11, I requested a meeting with Anne Pasternak to discuss my newest idea, Focus on Peace. And when she asked me why I hadn't come up with this idea six months earlier, I said I couldn't have. I was too busy mourning the loss of Lower Manhattan along with everyone else. When Anne promised partial sponsorship and sent me to Moukhtar Kococe at the Lower Manhattan Cultural Council, I'd found a new collaborator as well as a new sponsor. The LMCC lost its offices as well as one of its artists-in-residence in the World Trade Center attacks, and the organization has spent the past few years concentrating on healing and revitalizing their neighborhood through art and culture. It was in the moment that Moukhtar turned to me in our first meeting and said, "It's a call for prayer," and I replied, "Yes, without asking people to pray," that I became so touched by the opportunity just handed to me. I felt I might really contribute to healing my city and forced back the tears of gratitude for all that had allowed me to arrive at just this moment.

The press release read in part:

FOCUS ON PEACE BY NANCY BURSON,
A project of the Lower Manhattan Cultural Council in partnership with Creative Time, and with funding support from the Rockefeller Foundation.

Launches early September, 2002

This unique campaign will distribute 30,000 postcards and 7,000 posters inscribed with the message "Focus on Peace" around the anniversary of September 11.

Forming a visual pun, the gray text floating on a monochromatic background "Focus on Peace" is comprised of letters that are slightly out of focus. A message with optic, psychic and meditative dimensions, Burson elaborates in her artist statement:

"Focus on Peace" is a citywide declaration that serves as a visualization/contemplation tool to shift our consciousness forward. It is a positive action message of healing and hope.

What we see outside ourselves is a projection of what lies within. By asking people to "Focus on Peace," we are asking them to focus on their own personal peace within, as well as the concept of world peace. There can never be peace until we have peace within ourselves. Therefore, real peace consists of all the pieces.

By holding the frequency of peace we create the intention for it to manifest."

Arts and community-based groups, schools and universities as well as small businesses and storefronts Downtown will be invited to display "Focus on Peace" posters and postcards. These materials as well as email blasts will be distributed during the first week of September until supplies last.

For me, the whole idea of "Focus on Peace" was for the graphics to function as what one friend called "experiential phenomenology." In other words, I wanted people to read it and have trouble focusing on it. I believe it is in that 1 to 3 seconds of concentration that clarifies and promotes the viewer's own vision of peace, shifting one's attention from head to heart.

At the height of the Focus on Peace project, the

LMCC and I also collaborated in securing a spot to hang a monumental FOP scrim on one of the buildings whose perimeter was adjacent to the site. The crippled Deutsche Bank building, still vacant, was a likely candidate. Not only had they already hung a large American flag on the side overlooking the site, but as neighbors, Deutsche Bank had sponsored other project's of the LMCC's. Initially, the Deutsche Bank people were genuinely interested in hanging the scrim. In August of 2002, with the possibility of war with Iraq growing more likely, the Deutsche Bank executives reconsidered their decision. They were concerned about how it would be interpreted in light of the current political situation. Ironically, the American flag, which had been hanging there for the entire year, tore in half during the first anniversary ceremony from the sudden high winds that overtook the afternoon service. It remained there for at least another 10 days, a symbolic testament to a country divided.

A week before the anniversary of 9/11, I set out with the help of a few volunteers, and the help of the LMCC's Erin Donnally coordinating the effort, to the area surrounding the site of the World Trade Center. We came with hundreds of posters and postcards and

A view of Ground Zero, taken just before the anniversary of 9/11, with my proposed Focus on Peace scrim computer-generated to appear to be hanging on the crippled Deutsche Bank Building.

canvassed almost the entire area that week. We covered Tribeca, (named so because it is the TRIangle BElow CAnal Street), as well the area to the south of the site. We usually went in teams of two, giving shopkeepers the option of hanging a poster or postcard of Focus on Peace in their store windows for the upcoming anniversary.

Some of the storefronts on Chambers Street and farther south are tiny, appearing not much wider than the door itself. It was some of these store owners who were the most welcoming and enthusiastic. There were shopkeepers who were thrilled to have posters and postcards both. We also heard angry words filled with frustration and bitterness from some of those closest to Ground Zero. The variety of reactions of people stimulated by Focus on Peace created days of emotional extremes, highs and lows that were echoes of public opinion and broadcasts by the media.

When I went back a few days after the anniversary of 9/11, I found myself documenting in stills and videotape Tribeca only. I had no interest in visiting Ground Zero again. I had no interest in finding out how many of the cards and posters had been taken down.

In my mind the most compelling moment from

the project was a conversation I had with a couple of cops I'd followed into a bar a block from the site. I offered them a postcard and as good New York City cops and military veterans of the war in Bosnia, the response was, "Do you honestly think you can stop these guys by doing that?" And I said, "yes." Our discussion continued from there, and ultimately I realized neither side was going to budge. At the end of the conversation one of the officers said, "I want you to know I admire and respect what you're doing and God bless you for it. I just can't go there myself." And I said I felt exactly the same way, and that I also respected and understood how he felt and I thanked him for being there for New York City as well as Bosnia and I blessed him too.

What was most interesting about this conversation was that we were holding onto each other the whole time we were talking. Our arms had literally been linked. Ultimately, we had simply been human beings expressing ourselves. Even though we would never agree, the bottom line was more about our sameness, our commonality, our Beingness—not about our differences. We had been two arms outstretched toward the other and that very fact had united us, regardless of our beliefs.

Making a Difference

August 21, 2002 Houston Texas

Ten thousand people are attending a basketball game. Suddenly, one of the referees drops to the floor, victim of an apparent heart attack. As the crowd watches the referee lying lifeless on the floor of the arena, someone begins to recite "The Lord's Prayer." Ten thousand people, heads bowed in prayer, join together to focus on this man. The sportscasters are on their feet declaring they've never seen anything like it. And ultimately, the referee survives.

My question is, would this have happened before 9/11?

My beloved former assistant Kevin Johnson dropped his camera equipment and ran for his life that day. For years, he'd struggled with the dilemma of whether to pursue a career in art, or do something in the field of law enforcement. Now he's a New York City cop.

I am grateful for the gains we as human beings have made since the shake-up call of 9/11. I believe we have all shifted. We are more in our hearts and we are more tender toward one another. I have blessed the souls who lost their lives that day and I thank them for being in service to what I believe is the beginning of the paradigm shift in human consciousness from "I-ness" (concern for self) to "We-ness" (concern for all). There is no doubt in my mind that global consciousness exists.

Every New Year's Eve for the past five years, Roger Nelson's "Eggs" have "gone off," meaning that the 60 random number generators registered significant non-random sequences. The global consciousness worldwide registered a unity of thinking or emotion on or around midnight in all thirty-seven time zones. Nelson believes it is that sharing of thought and emotion of being in a transitional moment that causes the effect. In terms of the bigger picture, Roger Nelson states, "It means that the earth cannot support us in comfort as things are now. It urges a new understanding that we must learn to accept each other and help and support each other everywhere in the world, if we are to live in peace on this beautiful earth."

FIVE

Live in Your Heart

WE HUMANS ARE LIVING IN THE MIDST OF A world in crisis. For Americans, almost none of us can make sense of the politics that have brought us to this irrational moment in our history. We mourn the simplicity of our lives before September 11. Let's not buy into the predictions of gloom and doom for the future. We can use light to combat darkness. Cast light upon darkness and only the shadows remain. Let us focus on peace. Let us focus on light and love. Let us maintain a focus of inner peace as a model for the world, because even if we focus on inner peace, it still affects the greater goal of oneness.

What can we Americans do? How can each of us make a difference in our world today? How can each of us affect the greater goal of consciousness? We can each change our own lives. We can each hold a focus, create an intention, say a prayer, of oneness, of wholeness, of connectedness. We can change our pattern of thinking and focus on more positive thoughts. Reverend Betsee Parker, the head chaplain at Ground Zero, gave birth to a healthy baby girl at the age of 51 last year. She and her husband named their baby Rose. She is one of six women associated with the Medical Examiner's office who gave birth after their work at the site.

Energy is conscious and all consciousness is energy. Geophysical researcher, John Burke says, "We're all in an electromagnetic dance with our planet on a daily basis." Let us plug in and stay connected, to our selves and to each other. We're all part of the same power station. God, (or whatever way you refer to that energy) is the collective or unified field of consciousness or awareness. The best way to tune into our electromagnetic universe is to focus. Through our energy we can create peace. We are all one race, the human race. We are one nationality called humanity. Through our hearts, we can become one collective heart.

Ultimately, our quality of life is determined by

how much love we can give . . . to ourselves, to each other, to the people passing by us on the street. No matter how caught up we are in our own lives, what is truly significant is how much light we have the capacity to pour into our etheric bank accounts. The light that we hold in our bodies is a reflection of how much love we can give. If we open our hearts we can expand our love endlessly for ourselves and each other. It is that and that alone that comprises how much we love ourselves, each other, the human race and planet Earth. It is our capacity to open our hearts that determines our happiness. All that we have is now, in this moment.

A few years ago I saved an E-mail that I thought was so important that I cut it out and put it in my wallet. It is from A Course in Miracles, and it says, "Every action is either an expression of love or a call for love." David Deida, who writes and teaches extensively about relationships, tells us that if we're not doing love, we're doing fear. When we're not present to give our love fully, everyone we have a relationship with feels it, knows it, and is hurt by it. On the other hand, "When you live as love, then you give love to the world resonating others so they too, open and begin to live as love."

How can we tell when we are in our hearts?

We are in our hearts when we stroke our pets, when we smile and want to touch every baby we see, and when we focus on changing the expression on the face of the person who packs up our groceries, or who sells us a Metro card.

Our hearts are open whenever and wherever we're singing or dancing, as well as when we're making love, or laughing until we weep.

It is these small gifts of pure love from our hearts that have such a profound effect on us all. They translate into the same global connectedness that registers shifts in consciousness worldwide. In the Spring 2003, both the formalized "end" of the war in Iraq and the terrorist bombings in Riyadh and Casablanca registered significant readings on Roger Nelson's random number generators, or EGGs. They continue to provide us with proof that our global heartbeat can and does align.

If each of us had an hour left to live, how would we want to live that hour? We can choose. And, for that matter, we can choose every ten seconds. Will it be happiness or drama, love or anger? Can we move

Energy, seen as orbs, captured in this photograph taken of a wheat field in Wiltshire, England

beyond the conflicting, inconsistent images of our past and simply be and feel love? This is our task on planet earth in this moment, and it is humanity's challenge now. Let us choose light. Let us choose love. Let us choose to focus.

Ways to Focus

1. Use your closed eyes like a screen. Focus on the images that come up for you. How do these images impact on the thousands of thoughts we have each day? Are they positive or negative?

2. Lighten the energy around you by asking "Who does this belong to?" Recognize it's not yours and it will leave. If you asked yourself this question repeatedly over the course of one day, you'll become very aware of what is and isn't yours.

3. Cancel negative thoughts, and say or think them over again differently. Practice removing negative words from your vocabulary.

4. Analyze your judgements against yourself and others.

5. Three-five minutes of focusing . . . a) Focus on your breath and follow it. b) Connect to Source by bringing light down through you and down deeply into the earth. c) Pull energy from above and below us and connect it at the heart. d) Inhale love and light and exhale anger, pain, resentment, etc. e) Be the connector between heaven and earth and pull the energy of the earth's core up though you and the universe down into you connecting them at your heart.

6. Determine how you intuit energy. Are you a see-er, hearer, feeler, or knower?

7. Raise your own frequency by practicing bringing energy into yourself though seeing it or feeling it by yourself, or with a partner.

8. Bless those you don't agree with or like. They serve as mirrors and chances are they're reflecting some aspect of yourself that's a part of you as well. Use the simple techniques described to forgive yourself and others.

9. Send love in and out of your heart, to yourself, to other's, to the people of planet earth. Consciously focus on your own inner peace as a model for the world.

Recommended Books and Websites

Recommended Books

David Deida, *It's A Guy Thing, An Owner's Manual for Women* (Health Communications, 1997). Women, read this book. It will really shift your relationship to yourself, your mate and everyone else in your life.

David Deida, *The Way of the Superior Man, A Spiritual Guide to Mastering the Challenges of Women, Work, and Sexual Desire* (Plexus, 1997). Men, read this book. It will really shift your relationship to yourself, your mate and everyone else in your life. Deida is a brilliant master on the relationship between the sexes and opening and loving from the heart.

Masaru Emoto, *The Message From Water: Telling Us to Take a Look at Ourselves*, Volume I and Volume II.
The experience of Japanese researchers who studied how water crystals are affected by and respond to words and music.

Louise L. Hay, *You Can Heal Your Life* (Santa Monica, California: Hay House, 1987). A truly valuable book to accompany you through the journey of self love and acceptance. It includes the well-known list of ailments and affirmations to heal old thought patterns.

FOCUS

Jane Katra, Ph.D. and Russell Targ, *The Heart of the Mind, How to Experience God Without Belief* (Novato, California: New World Library, 1999). Russell Targ, one of the inventors of remote viewing and Jane Katra discuss the intersection between mysticism and parapsychology. With a foreword by Marianne Williamson.

Kyriacos Markides *Riding With the Lion, In Search of Mystical Christianity*. Markides examines Christian mysticism and its connections to the Eastern and Western esoteric traditions through the monks of Mount Athos.

Lynn McTaggert, *The Field, The Quest for the Secret Force of the Universe*, (New York: Quill, 2003). The profound compilation of the link between physics and faith is memorable.

Albert Taylor *Soul Traveler, A Guide to Out-of-Body Experiences and the Wonders Beyond* (New York: New American Library, 2000). An engineer and researcher for NASA explains and teaches out of body experience.

Recommended Websites

www.starrfu.com   Starr Fuentes and the Casa Alma
   Retreat Center website

www.jodiserota.com   Jodi Serota's website

www.accessraz.com   Access and Gary Douglas website

www.moretruthwillsetyoufree.com   Derek O'Neill's
   website

www.newrealitiestv.com   Alan Steinfeld's website for
   purchase of videotapes

http://www.emerald-energies.com/   A site which allows
   you to see videotapes through the internet.

http://noosphere.princeton.edu   The Global Consciousness Project website

Acknowledgments

My thanks to Byron Preiss and Roger Cooper for their vision and guidance in this project and to Judy Gitenstein, my editor, who magically integrated the material.

My profound gratitude to Starr Fuentes, Jodi Serota, Gary Douglas, and Derek O'Neill who assisted in guiding me to the realizations that are reflected in this book. It is through them that I have learned the empowerment of self love and its expansion to others. I am honored that they are such a big part of my heart and my collective family.

Special thanks to Alan Steinfeld, who is not only a consistent resource of information on my community, but who shifted our lives in July 2003, when he lovingly brought us the orbs.

Special thanks as well to the remarkable healing genius of Victor Dyment, who is steadfast in his commitment to bring true physical health to me and my family, and thanks as well to his unique Russian frequency which has so profoundly changed our lives.

Many thanks to David Kramlich for his contribution both in co-parenting and compositing.

A special appreciation to Starr Fuentes, Maika Pollack, Jeanne McDermott, Clayton Maxwell, and Ann Marie Keating for their valuable early input on the text.

My thanks to my loving assistants Jordan Reznick,

Ersellia Ferron, Jaclyn Mayer, and Katie Weisberger, whose input and support were always helpful. Added thanks to Jaclyn Mayer for her assistance in the design of the FOP project.

My gratitude to Jack Woody, publisher of two of my photo books and master of design, for his early input on the Focus on Peace project and its translation into a book cover.

Special thanks to Meryl Hershey Beck who has provided us with truly transformational journeys, and who is always there with a grid or a giggle. My gratitude to Susan Burns for her memorable meditations and artful energetic wisdom. My Blessings to Ann Marie Keating for her loving radiance and profound knowledge of conscious partnership. Thanks to Phil Gruber, the wizard genius of metaphysics, for his enlightening comparisons of the ever-expanding, multi-dimensional universes, with the familiarity of vintage TV. Special thanks to Melissa Love for her grace, and her incredible children who spent so much time distributing the Focus on Peace images downtown. My gratitude to Jon Adolphe, Dalia Basiouny, Maxi Cohen, Daria DiBennardo, Abigail Hastings, O'Mara Leary, Cristina Loving, Nancy Mayans, Jeanne McDermott, Sean Morton, Rob Robb, and Dick Waterman, whose enduring friendships and healing presence are so valued. Thanks as well to Roger Nelson and John Burke for their willingness to share their knowledge of the universe.

FOCUS

Thanks to so many others for their healing contributions in my life, including Kyriacos Markides, Nancy Johnson, Ann Williams, Barbara Baer, Josie Lismay, Robert Jaffe, Melvin Leifert, Mark Breiner, Marty Edelston, Kevin Dowling, Russell Burke, Harold McCoy, Marianne Somers, Barney Cosenza, Kandis Blakely, Madeline Lockwood, Stephen Flores, Gwen Frey, Mary Beth Smith, Amma Narayani, Howard Wills, Peter Evans, Nelson Howe, Yeshi Dhonden, Konstantin Korotkov, Mitch Rabin, Anatoli Kashpirovski, Art Jackson, Selina Rodriguez, Sister Margaret Ellen Burke, Isabelle Kingston, Tim Barker, JP Farrell, Andrew Rubman, Rebecca Elmaleh, Robin Masci, Alan Handelsman, Simon Peter Fuller, Dain Heer, Kallista, Roger Gershon, Mark Naseck, Carol Cummings, Ed Barattini, Sabine Grandke, Michael Jascz, Jean DaSilva, David Deida and the NYC Deida Group.

My gratitude to Michael Julian Berz, my partner in love and trust, whose willingness to explore both the universe and his heart consistently reveals his courage and his openness to the path of conscious union. My thanks as well for Michael's expert knowledge of cameras, and his uncanny ability to photograph the veil.

My gratitude to my son, Keir Kramlich, who in unconditional love, is alternately my student and my teacher. I honor your vision and your humor. It is the presence of both these men in my life that allows me to refine the practice of loving open from my heart.

ABOUT THE AUTHOR

NANCY BURSON'S fourth and latest book, *Seeing and Believing: The Art of Nancy Burson*, (Twin Palms Press), was published in conjunction with her traveling retrospective of the same name. Her work has been shown in museums and galleries worldwide, including major exhibitions and installations at The International Center of Photography and the New Museum in New York City, The Venice Biennale, The Contemporary Arts Museum in Houston, and The Museum of Contemporary Photography in Chicago.

Best known for her pioneering work in morphing technology, enabling law enforcement officials to locate missing children and adults, she has recently received media attention for her Human Race Machine, which allows viewers to see themselves as a different race. There are now several Human Race Machines currently touring the U.S. college and university market. As a photographer, writer, inventor, healer, and minister, Burson has lectured and taught worldwide, including a visiting professorship at Harvard and an adjunct position at New York University.

In the last few years she has collaborated with Creative Time and the Lower Manhattan Cultural Council completing several important public art projects. These projects include the billboard "There's No Gene For Race" and the poster/postcard project "Focus on Peace." The LMCC's

"Focus on Peace" project distributed 30,000 postcards and 7,000 posters around the site of the World Trade Center to coincide with the anniversary of 9/11.

For further information, visit www.nancyburson.com and www.focusonpeace.net.